How to Draw the Life and Times of
Andrew Jackson

Melody S. Mis

The Rosen Publishing Group's
PowerKids Press™
New York

To Leonard Keller, a dear friend

Published in 2006 by The Rosen Publishing Group, Inc.
29 East 21st Street, New York, NY 10010

First Edition

Editor: Jennifer Way
Layout Design: Ginny Chu

Illustrations: All illustrations by Holly Cefrey.
Photo Credits: pp. 7, 10, 20 (right) Library of Congress Prints and Photographs Division; pp. 8 (left), 14 The Hermitage: Home of President Andrew Jackson, Nashville, TN; p.9 Courtesy of historicnashville.com; p. 16 daisyfield.com; p. 18 Courtesy of the Naval Historical Center; p. 20 (left) © Bettman/Corbis; p. 22 The Seminole Tribune; p. 24 Ginny Chu/The Rosen Publishing Group; p. 26 Independence National Historical Park; p. 28 U.S. Senate Collection.

Library of Congress Cataloging-in-Publication Data

Mis, Melody S.
How to draw the life and times of Andrew Jackson / Melody S. Mis.
    p. cm. — (A kid's guide to drawing the presidents of the United States of America)
Includes bibliographical references and index.
ISBN 1-4042-2984-1 (library binding)
1. Jackson, Andrew, 1767–1845—Juvenile literature. 2. Presidents—United States—Biography—Juvenile literature. 3. Drawing—Technique—Juvenile literature. I. Title. II. Series.

E382.M57 2006
973.5'6'092—dc22

2004016582

Manufactured in the United States of America

Contents

Andrew Jackson

In 1828, Andrew Jackson was elected the United States' seventh president. To many Americans he represented the common man because he came from a poor family and did not have a college education. As president, Jackson worked to  make the United States a more democratic nation.

Jackson was born on March 15, 1767, in the Waxhaw settlement on the border between North Carolina and South Carolina. Jackson attended school but he preferred playing to studying. When he was 13 years old, Jackson left school to fight the British during the American Revolution.

In 1784, Jackson began to study law in Salisbury, North Carolina. He moved to Nashville, Tennessee, in 1788 to practice law. It was there that Jackson met Rachel Donelson Robards, whom he married in 1791. In 1804, they purchased a home and farm near Nashville, which he called the Hermitage.

Between 1812 and 1818, Jackson became a national war hero. He won victories against the British in the War of 1812, which lasted from 1812 to 1815. Jackson and his militia also won victories against Native American nations in the Creek War, which lasted from 1813 to 1814. He also fought in the First Seminole War in 1818.

Jackson served in the U.S. Senate from 1823 to 1825. In 1828, Jackson beat President John Quincy Adams in the presidential election and served two terms as president.

You will need the following supplies to draw the life and times of Andrew Jackson:

✓ A sketch pad   ✓ An eraser   ✓ A pencil   ✓ A ruler

These are some of the shapes and drawing terms you need to know:

Horizontal Line	——	Squiggly Line	ᨋᨆ
Oval	⬭	Trapezoid	⬠
Rectangle	▭	Triangle	△
Shading	▰	Vertical Line	│
Slanted Line	/	Wavy Line	∿

Old Hickory

Andrew Jackson's battlefield victories had made him popular. Jackson's troops called him Old Hickory, because they thought he was as strong as a hickory tree. When Jackson ran for president in 1828, he used the hickory tree as his symbol.

Jackson was also known as the first frontier president because he came from the largely unsettled Tennessee territory. Because his family was poor and from the frontier, Jackson felt that he was one of the common people, like a farmer or a soldier.

During Jackson's eight years in office, he increased the powers of the president by using the presidential veto to stop legislation he did not think was good for the country. To veto something means to reject it.

As president, Jackson tried to carry out what he thought were the wishes of the people. Although he had many successes, Jackson sometimes treated others badly. The most harmful thing that Jackson did was to force the Native Americans off their land by signing the Indian Removal Act of 1830.

Andrew Jackson's roots on the Tennessee frontier appealed to many Americans. His military background secured his fame as an American war hero. C. Severin created this print of Jackson fighting in the Battle of New Orleans around 1856.

Jackson's Tennessee

Andrew Jackson's tomb (above left) is located at the Hermitage, outside Nashville, Tennessee. The tomb is similar to a Greek temple on wallpaper inside the home.

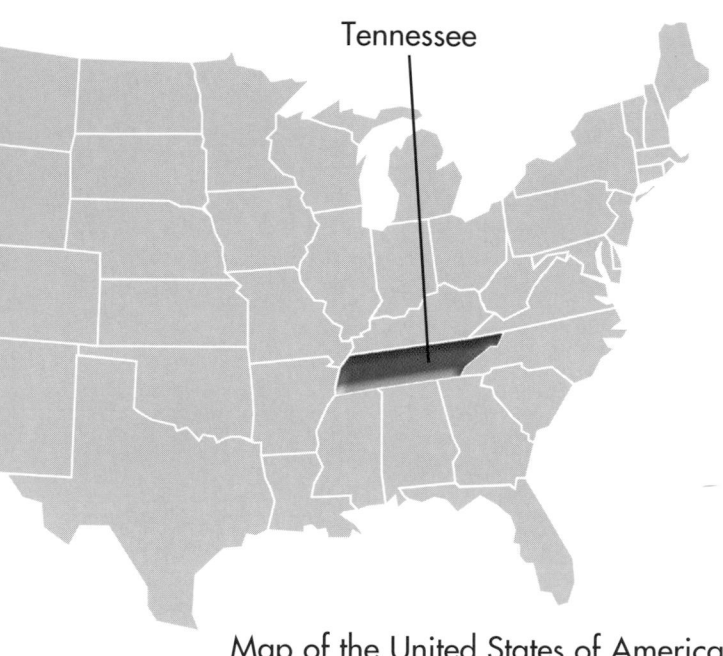

Map of the United States of America

Tennessee

Andrew Jackson spent most of his adult life in Tennessee. In 1788, he moved to Nashville where he later bought a home, which he called the Hermitage. Jackson made a name for himself in Tennessee by serving in the state government. He made Tennessee famous when he became the first person from that state to be elected president.

Tennessee honored Jackson's accomplishments by hiring the Nashville artist Clark Mills to create a bronze statue of the former president, which was revealed in 1880. The statue shows Jackson sitting

Clark Mills's statue of Jackson on a horse (above) is on the lawn of the Tennessee capitol in Nashville. There is also a copy of this statue in New Orleans, Louisiana. This statue celebrates Jackson's victory in the Battle of New Orleans.

on a horse that is rearing up on its back legs. It celebrates Jackson's victories on the battlefield. The statue is located in front of the state capitol building in Nashville.

When Jackson died in 1845, he was buried at the Hermitage in the tomb next to Rachel. American architect David Morrison created the tomb in 1831 in the style of a Greek temple. Greek temples are known for their columns. People today can visit the Tennessee capitol and the Hermitage to learn more about Andrew Jackson.

Andrew Jackson's Birthplace

Andrew Jackson was born on March 15, 1767, in a log cabin in the Waxhaw settlement on the border between North Carolina and South Carolina. He was the third child born to Andrew and Elizabeth Jackson. The Jacksons had moved from Ireland two years before Andrew's birth. The Carolina frontier, where the Jacksons settled, was home to many people who had emigrated from Ireland and Scotland.

Life on the frontier was hard. People had to grow their own food and build their own homes out of logs. Shortly before Andrew was born, his father died. After Andrew's birth, Elizabeth and her children went to live with her sister, Jane Crawford, and her family, who lived nearby. Although Jackson's original birthplace does not exist today, we know what the cabin looked like from pictures of it, like the one above.

1

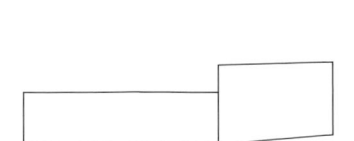

To begin drawing Jackson's birthplace, use a ruler to draw a rectangle and the other four-sided shape as shown.

2

Add the top of the house's side using two lines that meet at a point. Add lines for land. Draw the door and windows.

3

Draw the roof. Use two straight lines to begin a fence to the right side. Draw two windows and the vertical line on the side of the house. Add a step beneath the door.

4

Erase extra lines. Add a side to the fence. Draw the chimney. Add a barrel. Draw lines for logs on the house. Add three rectangles to the house and a line to the window on the right.

5

Erase extra lines. Add lines to the side of the house as shown. Draw logs on the roof. Draw a smaller chimney. Add a side to the larger chimney. Add ovals to the log ends.

6

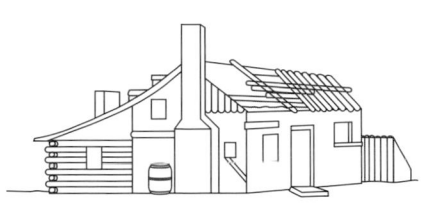

Erase extra lines. Add rings to the barrel. Draw lines on the fence and draw more logs on the roof. Draw two small shapes on the back of the roof. Add to the logs on the side.

7

Erase the lines of the logs that overlap. Draw vertical lines on the front and side of the house and on the fence. Add lines to the roof. Draw squiggly lines for the smoke from the chimney.

8

Erase extra lines. Finish with shading. Notice the areas that are shaded the darkest. Nice job!

Jackson and the American Revolution

Andrew Jackson was eight years old when the American Revolution began in 1775. From 1775 to 1777, Americans flew the

Grand Union flag, shown here. It was America's first flag. The cross in the corner was the same as Great Britain's flag. This was soon changed to stars so that the flag would not resemble Great Britain's flag.

In 1780, British soldiers killed more than 100 people living in the Waxhaw area. This made 13-year-old Jackson so angry that he joined a local militia and fought the British at the Battle of Hanging Rock in 1780. It was common at that time for boys his age to join the militia. In 1781, Jackson and his brother Robert were captured and sent to a prison in Camden, South Carolina. After his capture and before he was sent to prison, Jackson was ordered to polish a British soldier's boots. Jackson refused, and the soldier hit him with his sword. The cuts on Jackson's hand and face left scars that remained throughout his life.

1

Begin by drawing a rectangle. Draw the lines on the left side as shown. This is the edge of the flag.

2

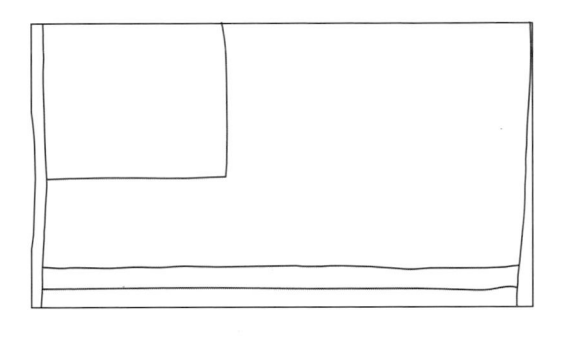

Draw a slanting line on the right side. Add two lines to complete a rectangle. This part of a flag is called a canton. Begin drawing lines across the flag to make stripes.

3

Erase the sides of the rectangle. Finish drawing the lines. There are 12 to make 13 stripes. Draw the cross shape inside the canton as shown.

4

Draw eight *V*'s. These form Britain's Union Jack. The *X*-shaped cross represents Scotland's St. Andrew's Cross. The other cross represents England's St. George's Cross.

5

Finish with shading. The triangles are very dark. There are seven dark stripes and six light ones. You have finished your Grand Union flag.

Meet Rachel Donelson Jackson

Rachel Donelson was born in Virginia in 1767. In 1785, Rachel wed Lewis Robards. It was an unhappy marriage, and the couple separated. Rachel went to live with her mother in Nashville. In 1788, Andrew Jackson began practicing law in Nashville and rented a room at Mrs.

Donelson's. Jackson and Rachel soon became friends.

In 1791, after Rachel heard that Robards had divorced her, she and Jackson got married. Two years later they learned that Robards had applied for a divorce, but that the divorce had not yet been granted. The divorce was finally granted in 1793, and Rachel and Jackson got married again a year later. This situation caused people to say bad things about the Jacksons during the 1828 presidential campaign. For the rest of his life, Jackson believed that the ugly talk caused Rachel to become ill and die on December 22, 1828, a few weeks before he took office as president.

1

Begin by drawing an oval for the head. This will be a guide that you will erase later. Draw a line for the neck and body. This will also be erased.

2

Draw guidelines for the eyes, nose, and mouth. Add a small oval for the ear. Draw the guidelines for the shoulders, arms, and hand.

3

Draw the outline of Rachel's body. Draw the jaw and cheek. Draw the hairline. Draw almond-shaped ovals for the eyes.

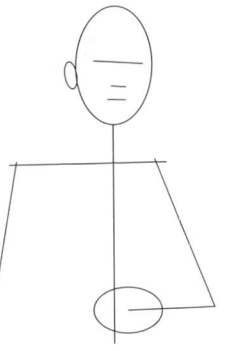

4

Erase the straight body guidelines, the head oval, and the eye guideline. Draw the nose and mouth as shown. Add the lines to the eyes and the ear. Draw the bonnet. Be sure to include the strings.

5

Erase the nose and mouth guidelines. Draw eyebrows. Add dots to the eyes. Draw the collar. Add lines to the face, ear, and neck. Draw the hand as shown. She is holding a necklace.

6

Erase the hand oval and the extra lines on the face, collar, bonnet, and body. Add lines to the eyes. Draw the dress and jewelry. Add two lines to the bonnet.

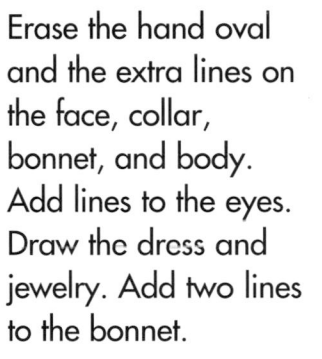

7

Add the lace to the bonnet. Erase the body outline and the lines of the jewelry that pass through the bonnet strings. Draw the rest of the jewelry as shown. Add a belt.

8

Erase the part of the belt that goes through the bonnet string. Finish with shading. The dress and the hair are very dark. Shade the background by using the side of your pencil tip.

The Hermitage

Andrew Jackson lived at the Hermitage in Nashville for more than 40 years. In 1804, he bought the property, which included a two-story cabin and more  than 600 acres (243 ha) of land. On part of the land Jackson grew cotton, which he sold. The rest of the land was used to grow food for the family, the slaves who worked on the farm, and the animals.

The Jacksons' home at the Hermitage began as a two-story log farmhouse. In 1821, Jackson and Rachel moved from the farmhouse into the larger brick home that Jackson had had built. In 1831, Jackson added to the house so that it included a library, an office, and a dining room. After a fire harmed the home in 1834, Jackson had it rebuilt and added columns to the front of the building. The state of Tennessee bought the Hermitage in 1856. Since then it has been restored and is open to the public.

1

Use a ruler to draw the rectangles as shown. These shapes will serve as the basis for your drawing of the Hermitage.

4

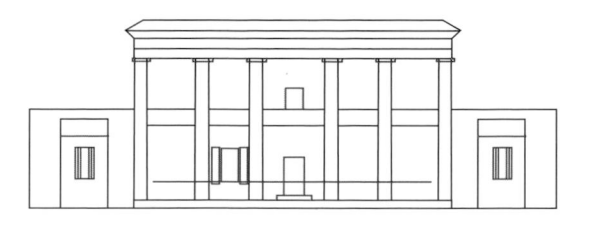

Erase extra lines. Add top edges to the columns. Draw a window on the second floor and detail lines to the side sections. Add a door in the center and a step. Draw a horizontal line on the first floor. This will be a guide for the first-floor windows. Draw a window with shutters.

2

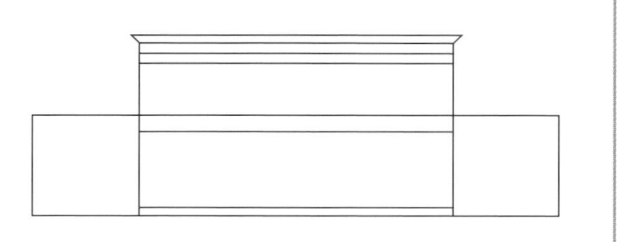

Draw the shape on top of the center rectangle. Notice how these lines flare slightly at either end. Draw four horizontal lines on the front of the building as shown.

5

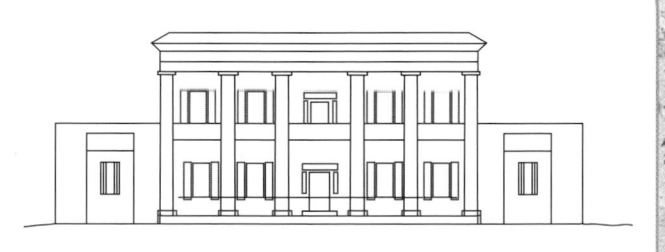

Draw the rest of the windows and shutters. Draw bottoms on the columns. Erase the tops of the columns that go through the edges. Add lines on the sides of the building for land. Add the shapes around the window and door you drew in step 4.

3

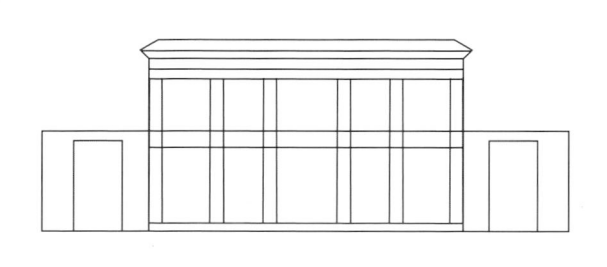

Draw another shape on the top of the center rectangle. This is the roof. Draw two shapes on the sides as shown. Draw six columns.

6

Erase the window guideline and extra lines in the bottom of the columns. Finish with shading. Make the windows and shutters very dark. The roof is dark, too. The columns are very light. Great job!

The War of 1812

Since the end of the American Revolution, the British navy had been capturing American ships. When the British navy fired on the American ship called the *Chesapeake* in 1807, the United States banned trade with Great Britain. The ban did not work, and the United States declared war on Britain in 1812. Andrew Jackson immediately offered to form a militia and fight.

During the first two years of the war, Jackson and his troops were not called upon to fight in the war. In December 1814, Jackson and his troops were sent to defend New Orleans, Louisiana, to defend the city from the British army. The Americans defeated the British army in January 1815. Because it took so long for news to reach people at that time, the British and Americans in New Orleans did not know that a peace treaty had been signed two weeks before the battle! However, the victory at the Battle of New Orleans made Jackson a national hero.

1

You will be drawing the *Chesapeake*. To begin, draw the body of the boat. Add a squiggly line for the water.

2

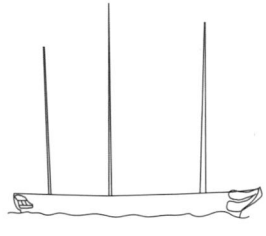

Draw three poles. Draw the back and front details on the boat body.

3

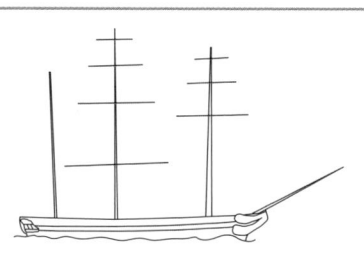

Erase extra lines. Draw two lines along the side of the boat. Draw lines across the poles as shown. The sails will hang from these. Draw a slanting pole on the front of the boat.

4

Draw sails on the front poles. Draw a line from the slanted pole to the boat. Add lines and a small shape on the back pole. Draw lines and a small shape on the boat's side.

5

Erase the pole that overlaps the front sail. Erase the top of the small shape. Add the canoe in back. Draw more sails and add ropes.

6

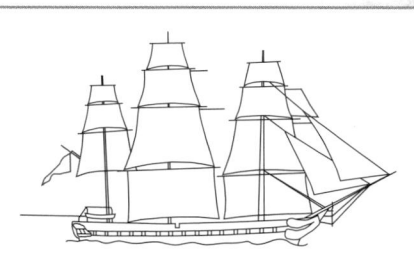

Erase extra lines. Draw ropes beneath the front pole. Draw more sails. Add lines next to some of the sails. Draw a flag and a pole at the back of the boat. Draw a line beneath it as shown.

7

Add the last sails. Erase the parts of the poles that go through the sails. Add detail lines to the boat. Add a long wavy flag on the middle pole. Draw squiggly lines for the water.

8

Finish with shading. The body of the boat is dark. The sails have light lines on them.

The Creek War

During the War of 1812, Jackson and his troops were sent to fight the Creek Native Americans. In 1813, the Creek had killed around 300 settlers at Fort Mims in Alabama. The Creeks were angry that white settlers were moving onto their lands. A group of Creek warriors called the Red Sticks wanted to protect their homeland. The Red Sticks' name came from the painted red clubs, or sticks, they used during battle.

One of the Red Sticks was called Menawa. He is shown above. Menawa was born in 1765. He led the Red Sticks against Jackson and his soldiers in the Battle of Horseshoe Bend on March 27, 1814. Jackson won the battle and forced the Creeks to sign the Treaty of Fort Jackson, ending the Creek War. The treaty said the Creeks had to move and give up half of their land to the United States. Today the Creeks are a tribal nation in Oklahoma. Their seal, shown above, was created in the nineteenth century.

1

You will be drawing the Muscogee Creek Seal. To begin draw two circles, one inside the other.

2 Add another circle very close to the bigger one. Inside the smaller circle, draw two diagonal lines. Draw an oval with a rectangle below it, as shown. At the bottom, add a curved line and a horizontal line that curves up at the end.

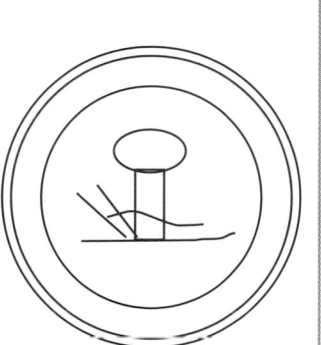

3

Draw the outline of the plow. Add the curved line near the top part of the rectangle.

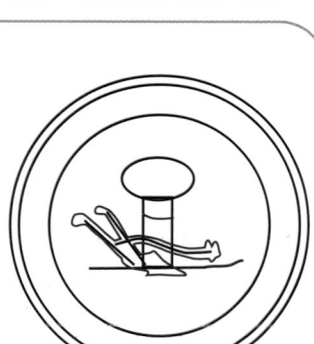

4

Erase the plow guidelines. Add details to the plow. Draw curved lines on the sides of the rectangle. Draw an oval around the curved line on the rectangle.

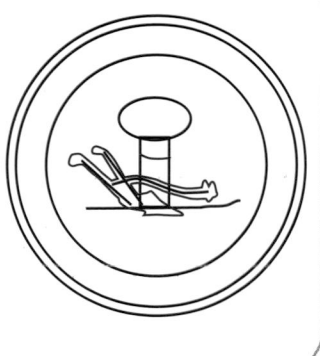

5

Erase extra lines. Draw squiggly lines around the oval. Add squiggly lines below the oval. Draw squiggly lines for the ground.

6

At the top of the circle write "GREAT SEAL OF THE."

7

Write the words "MUSCOGEE NATION I.T." at the bottom of the seal.

8

Finish with shading. Use squiggly lines to make the wheat, and use soft shading for the plow. Great job!

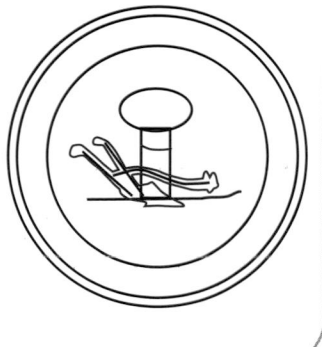

The First Seminole War

Early in the nineteenth century, the U.S. government thought the Seminole Native Americans were a threat to the United States. First the Seminoles had sided with the British

during the War of 1812. They were also taking in runaway slaves, which was against the law. The Seminoles lived in Florida in houses called chickees, like the one shown here.

In 1818, Andrew Jackson and his troops invaded Florida and defeated the Seminoles. They burned several Seminole settlements and captured the Spanish fort of Pensacola. These actions were done without official permission from the U.S. government. The invasion led Spain to believe that the United States wanted to take over Florida, which Spain controlled. To avoid conflict Spain sold Florida to the United States in 1819. President James Monroe appointed Jackson governor of Florida in 1821. Jackson was unhappy and quit after a few months.

1

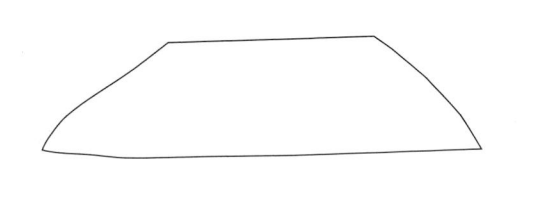

Draw the large shape as shown. This will be part of the roof of the chickee. Chickees have roofs but no walls. This makes it comfortable in Florida's hot weather.

2

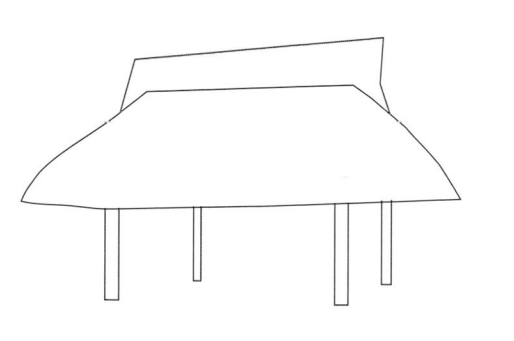

Add four poles using horizontal and vertical lines. Draw the shape on top of the roof as shown.

3

Draw the land at the bottom of the poles. The poles are buried in the ground to help give the house stability. Draw the line on the roof as shown. Draw a small upside-down *V* on the front.

4

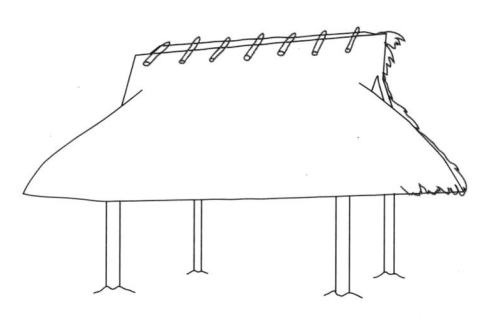

Erase the top part of the first roof shape. Draw sticks across the top of the roof. Draw squiggly lines for palm leaves as shown. Erase the bottom of the poles.

5

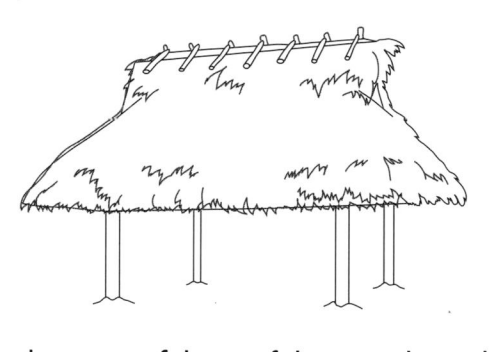

Erase the parts of the roof that run through the sticks and the palm leaves. Add small shapes to the top of the roof. These are the tops of the sticks on the other side of the roof. Finish drawing the palm leaves on the roof.

6

Erase the roof guide. Finish with shading. Use the side of your pencil to shade in the ground. Draw squiggly lines on the roof for palm leaves, and then lightly shade the roof in.

The Indian Removal Act of 1830

By the 1820s, American settlers were moving farther into southern lands that belonged to the Cherokee, Chocktaw, Creek, Chickasaw, and

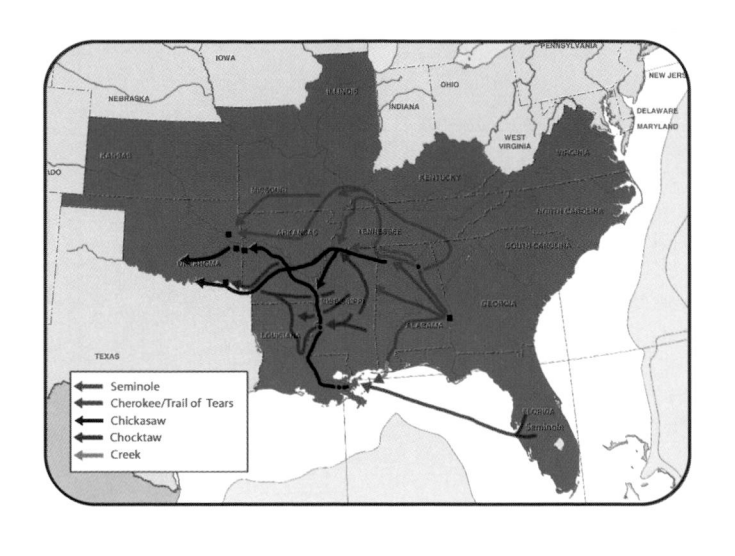

Seminole Native Americans. Fighting continued between the settlers and the Native Americans. The settlers pressed the U.S. government to take action.

Andrew Jackson, who had been elected president in 1828, felt that settlers had the right to move onto these lands. At that time Native Americans did not have any rights because they were not American citizens.

In 1830, Jackson signed the Indian Removal Act, which said that all Native Americans had to move to land west of the Mississippi River. During the move west, the Native Americans had to walk hundreds of miles. The routes they followed are shown in the map here. Many died on the journey. One example of this is the forced march of the Cherokee, which became known as the Trail of Tears.

1

You will be drawing a map that shows the routes that Native Americans took to Oklahoma. Begin by drawing a large rectangle. Use a ruler to divide it down the middle both ways.

2

Draw the squiggly line in the upper right rectangle as shown.

3

Draw the lines in the upper left rectangle as shown.

4

Draw the squiggly line in the lower left rectangle as shown.

5

Draw the lines and shapes in the bottom right rectangle. Begin drawing the state borders. Use the map on page 24 and the guidelines to see where your lines should go.

6

Finish drawing the state borders. Add lines in the upper right and the lower left boxes.

7

Add the lines and arrows as shown. These are the routes that the Natives Americans took when they were forced to move to Oklahoma.

8

Erase the guidelines. Finish by shading. Use the side of your pencil tip to shade in all the land. Shade the states in very dark.

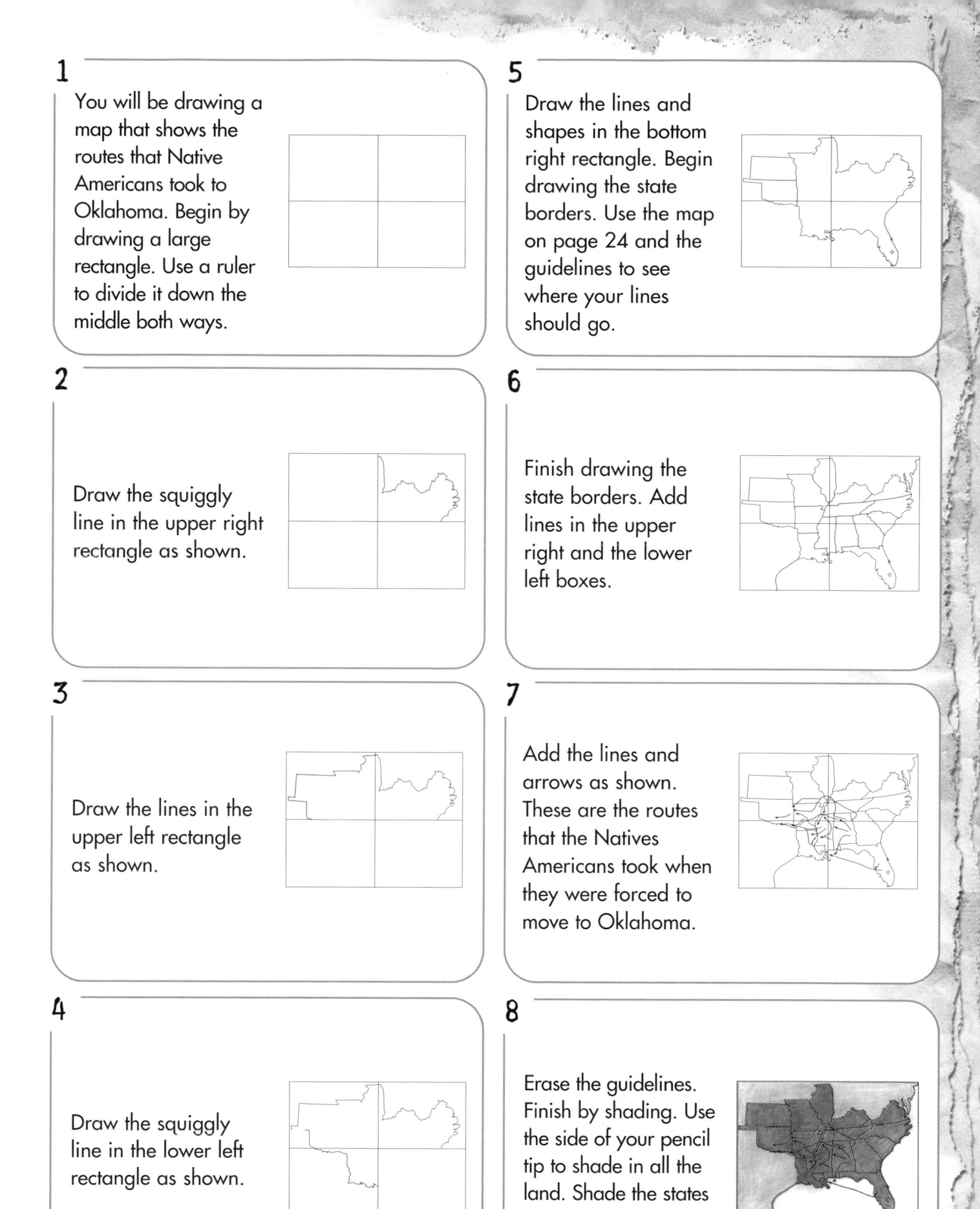

The U.S. Bank

The Second U.S. Bank was established in Philadelphia, Pennsylvania, by a charter in 1816. Its purpose was to hold a large amount of the

nation's money and to make loans to people or businesses. Wealthy businessmen had put up the money to get the bank started.

Andrew Jackson did not trust banks. He especially did not trust the U.S. Bank, because the government had no control over the bank. Jackson thought the bank had too much power and that it could use its power to hurt the country's economy.

Jackson won a second term as president in 1832. One of the main issues of the campaign was the upcoming renewal of the U.S. Bank's charter. Jackson vetoed the renewal of the bank's charter. This action caused the U.S. Bank to go out of business. Today the Second U.S. Bank building in Philadelphia, shown above, is a museum.

1

Begin by drawing a long horizontal line. Draw a rectangle that rests on the line. You have begun to draw the Second U.S. Bank building.

2

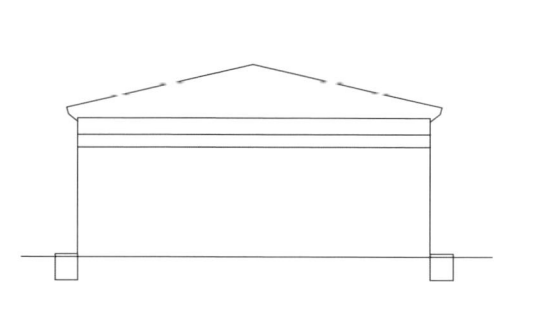

Draw the roof. Draw two horizontal lines across the front. Draw two small rectangles on the bottom. These rectangles drop below the horizontal line on either side of the building.

3

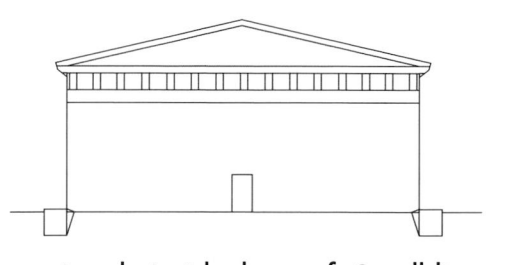

Draw a triangle inside the roof. Small lines extend from the bottom of the triangle to the roof and also from the top of the rectangle to the roof. Draw small vertical lines. Draw sides to the rectangles at the bottom and erase extra lines. Draw a door.

4

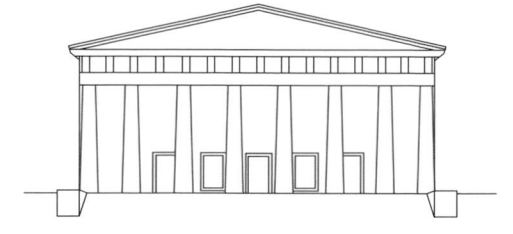

Erase extra lines in the square sides. Draw the lines on the roof. Draw eight columns across the front of the bank. They are slightly wider at the bottom. Draw more doors and detail lines between the columns.

5

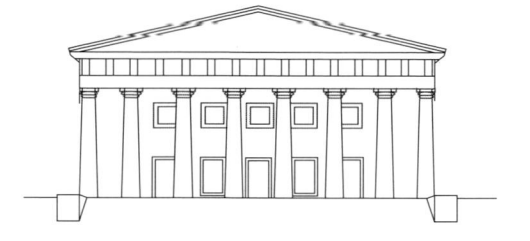

Erase part of the rectangle next to the columns. Add tops to the columns. Add the shapes between the columns.

6

Erase the parts of the columns that go through the tops. Erase the rest of the sides of the rectangle by the column tops, too. Finish with shading. Great job!

Jackson's Legacy

When Jackson's second term as president ended in 1837, he retired to the Hermitage. Jackson had health problems throughout his life, many of which were caused by wounds he received in battle. Jackson also suffered from tuberculosis, which is an illness of the lungs. On June 8, 1845, Andrew Jackson died at age 78.

Although Jackson had little education, he was a successful lawyer, military leader, and politician. Jackson is remembered as the first president to be born in a log cabin, the first president to come from the Tennessee frontier, and the first president to represent the Democratic Party. Jackson set an example for future presidential candidates by representing himself as one of the people, who had come from humble beginnings. He was the first president to pay off the national debt. The government honored Jackson for his popularity and his accomplishments when it put his face on the 20-dollar bill.

1

Begin your drawing of Andrew Jackson by making an oval for the head. This will be erased later. Draw a line for the neck and body.

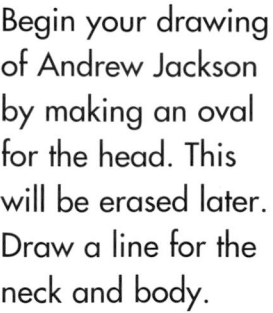

2

Draw guidelines for the eyes, nose, and mouth. Add an oval for the ear. Draw the neck and body outlines.

3

Erase the straight body guideline. Draw Jackson's jaw and chin. Draw almond-shaped ovals for the eyes. Draw the nose and mouth. Draw the collar of his shirt.

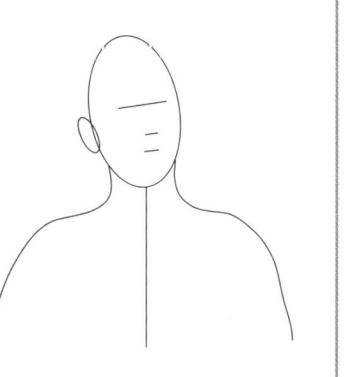

4

Erase extra lines. Draw the eyebrows. Add circles and lines to the eyes. Draw the hair and ear. Draw lines on his chin and around his mouth. Draw the large collar of his jacket.

5

Erase the head and ear ovals. Erase the body lines that go through the collar. Draw the rest of the hair. Add more lines to the face and eyes. Draw his shoulders.

6

Erase the body lines. Finish with shading, making his coat very dark. You can shade in the background by using the side of your pencil tip. You've just drawn Old Hickory. Nicely done!

Timeline

1767 Andrew Jackson is born in South Carolina.

1780–1781 Jackson is captured and put in prison during the American Revolution.

1784–1787 Jackson studies law.

1796 Jackson is elected to the U.S. House of Representatives.

1798–1804 Jackson serves as judge of the Tennessee Superior Court.

1802 Jackson is elected major general of the Tennessee Militia.

1804 Jackson purchases the Hermitage.

1812–1815 The United States fights Great Britain in the War of 1812.

1813–1814 Jackson and the Tennessee militia fight the Creek War.

1814 Jackson and his troops defeat the Creek Indians at the Battle of Horseshoe Bend.

1815 Jackson defeats the British at the Battle of New Orleans.

1818 Jackson defeats the Seminole Indians in Spanish Florida.

1823–1825 Jackson serves as a U.S. senator.

1828 Jackson is elected president.
Rachel Jackson dies.

1829 Jackson takes office as the nation's seventh president.

1830 Jackson signs the Indian Removal Act.

1832 Jackson vetoes the renewal of the Second U.S. Bank's charter.
Jackson is elected for a second term as president.

1837 Jackson retires to Nashville.

1845 Jackson dies at the Hermitage.

Glossary

American Revolution (uh-MER-uh-ken reh-vuh-LOO-shun) Battles that soldiers from the colonies fought against Britain for freedom, from 1775 to 1783.

architect (AR-kih-tekt) Someone who creates ideas and plans for a building or an organization.

celebrates (SEH-luh-brayts) Honors.

charter (CHAR-tur) An official agreement giving someone permission to do something.

declared (dih-KLERD) Announced officially.

defeated (dih-FEET-ed) Lost against someone in a contest or battle.

defend (dih-FEND) To guard from harm.

democratic (deh-muh-KRA-tik) Having to do with a government that is run by the people who live under it.

emigrated (EH-mih-grayt-ed) To have left one's country to settle in another.

frontier (frun-TEER) The edge of a settled country, where the wilderness begins.

invaded (in-VAYD-ed) Entered a place in order to attack and conquer it.

lawyer (LOY-er) A person who gives advice about the law and who speaks for people in court.

legacy (LEH-guh-see) Something left behind by a person's actions.

militia (muh-LIH-shuh) A group of people who are trained and ready to fight when needed.

reject (rih-JEKT) To refuse to accept or do something.

restored (rih-STORD) Put back; returned to an earlier state.

scars (SKARZ) Marks left by healed cuts or sores.

symbol (SIM-buhl) An object or a picture that stands for something else.

threat (THREHT) A person or thing that may be harmful.

tomb (TOOM) A place where a dead person is buried.

Index

Web Sites

Due to the changing nature of Internet links, PowerKids Press has developed an online list of Web sites related to the subject of this book. This site is updated regularly. Please use this link to access the list:
www.powerkidslinks.com/kgdpusa/jackson/